S.H.E. EMERGED

LAUNCH THE VISION SIS!
AN INTERACTIVE
DEVOTIONAL

Chalimar Shree'

The Everyday Life Bible: Notes & Commentary by Joyce Meyer. First Edition: Faith Words. New York, NY 2020. Print.
https://www.youversion.com/apps/New International Version
https://www.youversion.com/apps/New King James Version
https://www.youversion.com/apps/King James Version

LWI Publishing Services

Contact info:
www.launchthevisionsis.com

email: launchthevisionsis@outlook.com

Printed in the United States of America
First Printing: March 2023

Welcome to

Launch The Vision Sis

An interactive devotional designed to help you on your journey of self-discovery. My prayer is that you will take this opportunity and take the first steps to finding your purpose while learning to live on purpose, while tapping into God's vison for your life. I do not believe we found each other by chance. God has placed this devotional in your hands for a purpose, and that purpose is you. It's your season for greatness and I want to see you win!!!!

Chalimar Shree'

*****You will notice I have included a lot of extra areas for you to take notes and make journal entries. This is because writing exactly what you receive from God is important. The Word says write the vision and make it plain.*****

Before we get started. Let me pray for you, sis.

Father in the name of Jesus I come to you interceding on behalf of the woman who has been divinely assigned to walk this journey. God I ask that you open her heart and mind to receive all that you have for her during this journey. I pray that the petitions of her heart are heard and known by you. You said in your Word to pray without ceasing and to pray until we receive your answer. Father give her the will to pray without ceasing and the wisdom and courage to declare a thing as if it already is. God I pray that my sister will receive and write the vision as you have given it, that it is made plain so that she may read it and run with it. God I thank you in advance for releasing her from a season of bareness. That she may be productive and walk boldly in her newness and reap the harvest of her labor. Father I proclaim financial freedom, spiritual healing, peace, prosperity, and renewed relationship with you. I pray that every generational curse is broken, that every curse spoken against her, and her family be returned to the sender void, that every unholy covenant is destroyed and that the God who answers with fire will show up on her behalf. I declare, decree and proclaim these things to be so if it's your will they're already done.

In the mighty and matchless name of Jesus, Amen

Getting started:

The: Am I The Vision Board?

This vision board exercise is optional; however, I highly recommend you do it. Creating a vision board before you start to document your plans, will allow you the opportunity to reflect on how God's vision changes things.

30 Day Devotional

Each day includes:
Daily Devotional
Morning Prayer Entry
Morning Gratitude
Daily Planner
Evening Prayer
Evening Journal Dump

Each Week Includes: 7-day Reflection

The Finish Line:

The: I Am Vision Board!

This vision board is completed at the end so that you can see what God's plan is for you.

Bonus Content:

Mental Health Minute
Mini Prayer Journal
5-Minute Meltdown
and more

Bonus Content can be found at:
www.savedhealedenough.com/bonus

20—VISION

God's Promise

In Him also we have obtained an inheritance, being predestined according to the purpose of Him who works all things according to the counsel of His will, that we who first trusted in Christ should be to the praise of His glory
Ephesians 1:11-12

We are all designed originals, created in God's perfect will with a set purpose according to His plan. You are predestined to receive the inheritance that He promised! The catch is ... you must get into alignment and relationship with Him. You need to trust His purpose to be revealed!

◆━━━━━━━━━◆

God I thank you for the plan and purpose you have already laid out for me and my life. Father I submit to your authority and come into alignment with your will and promise for my life. Amen

Morning Prayer

Date: _____

Scripture

My Prayer

Father I have faith you will:

God's Instructions:

_____

_____

_____

_____

Daily Planner

Things I need to accomplish today

- ○ _____
- ○ _____
- ○ _____
- ○ _____
- ○ _____
- ○ _____
- ○ _____
- ○ _____

Things I want to accomplish

Goals for Tomorrow

Challenges I am prepared to face

Evening Gratitude

Date: _____

Father Today I felt......

_____

_____

_____

Father I'm grateful for.....

_____

_____

_____

Father forgive me for.....

_____

_____

_____

Father as I close out today what can I do for you tomorrow...

_____

_____

_____

"The promise of God is my portion"

Evening Prayer

Date: _____

Scripture

My Prayer

Father I am believing you for:

God's Instructions:

_____
_____
_____
_____

Evening journal dump!!
Write, Release, Restart

The Strength To Endure

That He would grant you, according to the riches of His glory, to be strengthened with might through His Spirit in the inner man
Ephesians 3:16

Sis listen, how many times have we created an idea in our minds and ran with it? When it doesn't work out we become discouraged. When we become discouraged it's because we lack the strength to endure! I have learned that We must pray for the strength to face what's ahead and ask God to condition our mind, body, and spirit for the journey! God **did not** create us to fail, so failure is NOT of Him! It's time to build your endurance!

———◆———————————◆———

Father, your resources are limitless and your grace knows no bounds. Lord strengthen me from the inside out that I may overcome my present experiences and grant me the wisdom to endure those things to come and the revelation that I may have a better understanding of you! Amen

Morning Prayer

Date: _____

Scripture

My Prayer

Father I have faith you will:

God's Instructions:

_____

_____

_____

_____

Daily Planner

DATE:

Things I need to accomplish today

- _____
- _____
- _____
- _____
- _____
- _____
- _____
- _____

Things I want to accomplish

Challenges I am prepared to face

Goals for Tomorrow

Evening Gratitude

Date: _____

Father Today I felt......

_____

_____

_____

Father I'm grateful for.....

_____

_____

_____

Father forgive me for.....

_____

_____

_____

Father as I close out today what can I do for you tomorrow...

_____

_____

_____

"The promise of God is my portion"

Evening Prayer

Date: _____

Scripture

My Prayer

Father I am believing you for:

God's Instructions:

_____

_____

_____

_____

Evening journal dump!!
Write, Release, Restart

_____

_____

_____

_____

_____

_____

_____

_____

_____

_____

_____

Awaken Me

That Christ may dwell in your hearts through faith; that you, being rooted and grounded in love, may be able to comprehend with all the saints what is the width and length and depth and height- to know the love of Christ which passes knowledge; that you may be filled with all the fullness of God.
Ephesians 3:17-19

When we become accustomed to living a certain way, it can be hard to change. We create habits that become routine parts of our lives. We operate in these routines for so long that we start to move through life almost as if we are sleepwalking but when we are intentional about seeking, discovering and walking in the fullness of God's love for us, an awakening takes place and as our hearts and minds are opened so are our eyes! Seek God so that you may be awakened to see your destiny as He sees it!

———●———————————●———

Lord, make me fully alive in you so that I may experience the fullness of the destiny that you have planned for my life. Amen

Morning Prayer

Date: _____

Scripture

My Prayer

Father I have faith you will:

God's Instructions:

_____

_____

_____

_____

Daily Planner

Things I need to accomplish today

- ○ _____
- ○ _____
- ○ _____
- ○ _____
- ○ _____
- ○ _____
- ○ _____
- ○ _____

Things I want to accomplish

Challenges I am prepared to face

Goals for Tomorrow

Evening Gratitude

Date: _____

Father Today I felt......

_____
_____
_____

Father I'm grateful for.....

_____
_____
_____

Father forgive me for.....

_____
_____
_____

Father as I close out today what can I do for you tomorrow...

_____
_____
_____

"The promise of God is my portion"

Evening Prayer

Date: _____

Scripture

My Prayer

Father I am believing you for:

God's Instructions:

_____

_____

_____

_____

Evening journal dump!!
Write, Release, Restart

_____

_____

_____

_____

_____

_____

_____

_____

_____

_____

_____

_____

_____

The Reset

Then Peter said to them, "Repent, and let every one of you be baptized in the name of Jesus Christ for the remission of sins; and you shall receive the gift of the Holy Spirit. For the promise is to you and to your children, and to all who are afar off, as many as the Lord our God will call."
Acts 2:38-39

In order to fully come into alignment with all God has for you, you must first fully commit and submit. Like any relationship in order for you to have longevity, it must be built on a solid foundation. Honesty, trust and sincerity are the cornerstones of a great relationship. These things are just as important in your relationship with God. You must be honest with Him and truly seek His forgiveness in earnest and trust that He will love you despite any transgressions you may have committed. You must understand that His purpose for confession is never to shame or judge you but to free you from the burden of carrying those things so that you can make room for your gifts. He also wants us to know that His blessings are a generational reward. Your relationship with Him is the start of true generational wealth!

◆——————————◆

Father forgive me for my transgressions, cleanse my heart, clear my mind and free my spirit from the bondage of my mistakes and errors in judgment. I am ready for my divine reset and I know your Grace is sufficient not just for me but for my bloodline. Amen

Morning Prayer

Date: _____

Scripture

My Prayer

Father I have faith you will:

God's Instructions:

_____
_____
_____
_____
_____

DATE:

Daily Planner

Things I want to accomplish

Things I need to accomplish today

- ◯ _____
- ◯ _____
- ◯ _____
- ◯ _____
- ◯ _____
- ◯ _____
- ◯ _____
- ◯ _____

Challenges I am prepared to face

Goals for Tomorrow

Evening Gratitude

Date: _____

Father Today I felt......

_____
_____
_____

Father I'm grateful for.....

_____
_____
_____

Father forgive me for.....

_____
_____
_____

Father as I close out today what can I do for you tomorrow...

_____
_____
_____

"The promise of God is my portion"

Evening Prayer

Date: _____

Scripture

My Prayer

Father I am believing you for:

God's Instructions:

_____
_____
_____
_____

Evening journal dump!!
Write, Release, Restart

_____

_____

_____

_____

_____

_____

_____

_____

_____

_____

_____

_____

No Fear

Peace I leave with you; my peace I give you. I do not give to you as the world gives.
Do not let your hearts be troubled and do not be afraid.
John 14:27

Sis in order to begin the journey of walking in your promise, aside from nurturing your relationship with God, you must also be actively working on your relationship with yourself. Launching God's vision for your life will require you to be both spiritually healthy and mentally healthy. You must start the process of reconditioning your mind not to hold onto things that stress you out and not to be intimidated or fearful of walking into the unknown. How many times have we taken a chance on things far less promising? It costs you nothing to take a chance on God's heart for you.

◆————————◆

Lord I'm tired and weary from carrying the pain of yesterday, the stress of today and the fear of what's to come. Father today I rest in you. I give you my troubles. Help me to not walk in fear but to be confident in you and trust you in all things and all ways. Amen

Morning Prayer

Date: _____

Scripture

My Prayer

Father I have faith you will:

God's Instructions:

_____

_____

_____

_____

DATE:

Daily Planner

Things I need to accomplish today

- ○ _____
- ○ _____
- ○ _____
- ○ _____
- ○ _____
- ○ _____
- ○ _____
- ○ _____

Things I want to accomplish

Goals for Tomorrow

Challenges I am prepared to face

Evening Gratitude

Date: _____

Father Today I felt......

_____

_____

_____

Father I'm grateful for.....

_____

_____

_____

Father forgive me for.....

_____

_____

_____

Father as I close out today what can I do for you tomorrow...

_____

_____

_____

"The promise of God is my portion"

Evening Prayer

Date: _____

Scripture

My Prayer

Father I am believing you for:

God's Instructions:

_____

_____

_____

_____

Evening journal dump!!
Write, Release, Restart

_____

_____

_____

_____

_____

_____

_____

_____

_____

_____

_____

_____

_____

_____

Write The Vision

Then the LORD answered me and said: "Write the vision, and make it plain on tablets, that he may run who reads it."
Habakkuk 2:2

DAY

Now let's be clear, research and planning are the core components to launching God's vision for your life. As God starts to reveal the vison to you, write it down, then research it. Make detailed lists of what you will need and how you will need to execute each item. You will need to be strategic not just in your planning but in your prayer life. Bring each item to God in prayer and wait for clarification. Take your time, there is no rush. God's timing is the best timing, and He has already laid out the plan, He was just waiting on you!

◆────────────◆

Lord, I am available to you, your humble servant. Hear my heart and make plain to me what it is you would have me to do? Make plain to me the vision that you have for me and grant me the wisdom to execute and walk in it so that you get the Glory. Amen

Morning Prayer

Date: _____

Scripture

My Prayer

Father I have faith you will:

God's Instructions:

_____

_____

_____

_____

Daily Planner

DATE:

Things I need to accomplish today

- ○ _____
- ○ _____
- ○ _____
- ○ _____
- ○ _____
- ○ _____
- ○ _____
- ○ _____

Things I want to accomplish

Goals for Tomorrow

Challenges I am prepared to face

Evening Gratitude

Date: _____

Father Today I felt......

_____
_____
_____

Father I'm grateful for.....

_____
_____
_____

Father forgive me for.....

_____
_____
_____

Father as I close out today what can I do for you tomorrow...

_____
_____
_____

"The promise of God is my portion"

Evening Prayer

Date: _____

Scripture

My Prayer

Father I am believing you for:

God's Instructions:

_____

_____

_____

_____

Evening journal dump!!
Write, Release, Restart

_____

_____

_____

_____

_____

_____

_____

_____

_____

_____

_____

_____

Your Circle

DAY

Now, my good sis, you must know that everyone cannot go where you are going and every "friend" will not be excited for you. As you begin to embark on this journey, prepare your heart and mind to lose some people and to gain some people. As you transition into this new season, your needs will change and it will impact your current social dynamic. It's ok to outgrow people, some are only meant to be in our lives for a season.

Father grant me the discernment to see who is meant for me and who is not. Lord remove anyone that may hinder my walk with you. I am trusting you to create divine connections with those who are meant to be with me on this journey, in this season. Amen

Morning Prayer

Date: _____

Scripture

My Prayer

Father I have faith you will:

God's Instructions:

_____
_____
_____
_____

DATE:

Daily Planner

Things I need to accomplish today

- ○ _____
- ○ _____
- ○ _____
- ○ _____
- ○ _____
- ○ _____
- ○ _____
- ○ _____

Things I want to accomplish

Challenges I am prepared to face

Goals for Tomorrow

Evening Gratitude

Date: _____

Father Today I felt......

_____

_____

_____

Father I'm grateful for.....

_____

_____

_____

Father forgive me for.....

_____

_____

_____

Father as I close out today what can I do for you tomorrow...

_____

_____

_____

"The promise of God is my portion"

Evening Prayer

Date: _____

Scripture

My Prayer

Father I am believing you for:

God's Instructions:

_____

_____

_____

_____

Evening journal dump!!
Write, Release, Restart

_____

_____

_____

_____

_____

_____

_____

_____

_____

_____

_____

_____

7 Days 7

reflections

MONDAY

TUESDAY

WEDNESDAY

THURSDAY

FRIDAY

SATURDAY

SUNDAY

When Temptation Comes

No temptation has overtaken you except such as is common to man; but God is faithful, who will not allow you to be tempted beyond what you are able, but with the temptation will also make the way of escape, that you may be able to bear it.
1 Corinthians 10:13

Real talk, there have been many days on my own journey that I have been tempted to run in the opposite direction that God was steering me. I just didn't want to do it! I was looking at the lives of those around me and it just looked easier to do it the way they were doing it. I realized that they too had their own process and as tempting as it was to want to follow them, God made it clear to me that His promise for them was NOT His promise me! My process was unique to the vision He had for me. God is as intentional in His choice of vision for our lives as He was in His creation of everything on this earth. One solution cannot address every problem and every vision cannot fit every visionary!

———◆———

Lord I trust you in all your ways. Redirect my thoughts when temptation is knocking on my mind's door. Remove any distraction that may lead me to temptation. Amen

Morning Prayer

Date: _____

Scripture

My Prayer

Father I have faith you will:

God's Instructions:

_____
_____
_____
_____

DATE:

Daily Planner

Things I want to accomplish

Things I need to accomplish today

- ◯ _____
- ◯ _____
- ◯ _____
- ◯ _____
- ◯ _____
- ◯ _____
- ◯ _____
- ◯ _____

Challenges I am prepared to face

Goals for Tomorrow

Evening Gratitude

Date: _____

Father Today I felt......

_____

_____

_____

Father I'm grateful for.....

_____

_____

_____

Father forgive me for.....

_____

_____

_____

Father as I close out today what can I do for you tomorrow...

_____

_____

_____

"The promise of God is my portion"

Evening Prayer

Date: _____

Scripture

My Prayer

Father I am believing you for:

God's Instructions:

_____

_____

_____

_____

Evening journal dump!!
Write, Release, Restart

_____

_____

_____

_____

_____

_____

_____

_____

_____

_____

_____

_____

_____

_____

_____

The Difference in Making a Difference

Now Deborah, a prophetess, the wife of Lapidoth, was judging Israel at that time. And she would sit under the palm tree of Deborah between Ramah and Bethel in the mountains of Ephraim. And the children of Israel came up to her for judgment.
Judges 4:4-5

Now for context, before Israel had kings they relied on judges. This was a position that required bravery and integrity. It was also a position that was historically held by men. Deborah clearly trusted God's vision for her life to step into such a non-traditional role for a woman. Her courage and faith speaks for itself as she would go on to not only save her people but to also forge into battle alongside of them. She had faith and knew that God had gone ahead of them in the battle. God's vision for our lives may not always be what we expect or are familiar with. It may not even be something that has been done before but that's ok. **Just because it hasn't been done doesn't mean YOU shouldn't do it or can't do it!!!** It just means YOU will be the blueprint for those who come after you!

◆————————◆

Lord thank you for allowing me to be the difference in making a difference. Thank you for choosing and trusting me with this vision that I may pour into others and be effective in every area of my life. Amen

Morning Prayer

Date: _____

Scripture:

Father I have faith you will:

My Prayer for revelation

What God Said:

_____

_____

_____

_____

_____

_____

_____

DATE:

Daily Planner

Things I want to accomplish

Things I need to accomplish today

- ○ _____
- ○ _____
- ○ _____
- ○ _____
- ○ _____
- ○ _____
- ○ _____
- ○ _____

Challenges I am prepared to face

Goals for Tomorrow

Evening Gratitude

Date: _____

Father Today I felt......

_____

_____

_____

Father I'm grateful for.....

_____

_____

_____

Father forgive me for.....

_____

_____

_____

Father as I close out today what can I do for you tomorrow...

_____

_____

_____

"The promise of God is my portion"

Evening Prayer

Date: _____

Scripture:

Father I am believing for:

My Prayer

What God Said:

_____

_____

_____

_____

_____

_____

_____

_____

Evening journal dump!!
Write, Release, Restart

_____

_____

_____

_____

_____

_____

_____

_____

_____

_____

_____

_____

_____

_____

Your Seat At The Table

"For if you remain completely silent at this time, relief and deliverance will arise for the Jews from another place, but you and your father's house will perish. Yet who knows whether you have come to the kingdom for such a time as this?"
Esther 4:14

This text is about Esther, a woman who did not seek leadership, but that was God's vison for her life. She was hesitant and didn't want to move forward with the assignment. After seeking God through fasting and prayer, she would eventually move forward in her assignment and save her people from impending doom! However, the text above makes it clear that although God wants you to be a part of the plan however His plans are NOT dependent on you so if you decide that you are not willing to walk in the vision He has for you, it won't be because he didn't believe you could but because you didn't believe he would!

———◆————————◆———

Lord settle in my spirit that I am worthy. Father clear any doubt that may arise. I know I may not have chosen this path but I understand that I am chosen and what's for me is for me. Lord remind me that I am who you say I am.. Amen

Morning Prayer

Date: _____

Scripture:

Father I have faith you will:

My Prayer for revelation

What God Said:

_____

_____

_____

_____

_____

_____

_____

Daily Planner

DATE:

Things I want to accomplish

Things I need to accomplish today

- ◯ _____
- ◯ _____
- ◯ _____
- ◯ _____
- ◯ _____
- ◯ _____
- ◯ _____
- ◯ _____

Challenges I am prepared to face

Goals for Tomorrow

Evening Gratitude

Date: _____

Father Today I felt......

_____

_____

_____

Father I'm grateful for.....

_____

_____

_____

Father forgive me for.....

_____

_____

_____

Father as I close out today what can I do for you tomorrow...

_____

_____

_____

"The promise of God is my portion"

Evening Prayer

Date: _____

Scripture:

Father I am believing for:

My Prayer

What God Said:

_____

_____

_____

_____

_____

_____

_____

Evening journal dump!!
Write, Release, Restart

_____

_____

_____

_____

_____

_____

_____

_____

_____

_____

_____

_____

_____

God Chose You

Then the woman of Samaria said to Him, "How is it that You, being a Jew, ask a drink from me, a Samaritan woman?" For Jews have no dealings with Samaritans. Jesus answered and said to her, "If you knew the gift of God, and who it is who says to you, 'Give Me a drink,' you would have asked Him, and He would have given you living water."
John 4:9-10

This is by far one of my favorite depictions of God's grace for us. This woman was the epitome of messy!! She was divorced 5 times and living with a man that was not her husband. Despite all of those things, Jesus did not hesitate to pour into her and use her to spread the gospel. He didn't wait for her to "get right", clean up her past, or raised her rank in society. In that moment she was a willing vessel and He saw fit to use her. If you start to feel like an imposter or unqualified because some say you lack certain qualifications, remember God does not call the qualified, He qualifies the called!

◆———————◆

Father help me to become confident in who you called me to be. Lord I am ready to receive your divine instructions so that I may know and understand what you have qualified me to do. Father guard my ear gates, my eye gates and my heart so that I will not be discouraged by those that try to discourage me. Amen

Morning Prayer

Date: _____

Scripture:

Father I have faith you will:

My Prayer for revelation

What God Said:

_____

_____

_____

_____

_____

_____

_____

Daily Planner

Things I need to accomplish today

- _____
- _____
- _____
- _____
- _____
- _____
- _____
- _____

Things I want to accomplish

Challenges I am prepared to face

Goals for Tomorrow

Evening Gratitude

Date: _____

Father Today I felt......

_____
_____
_____

Father I'm grateful for.....

_____
_____
_____

Father forgive me for.....

_____
_____
_____

Father as I close out today what can I do for you tomorrow...

_____
_____
_____

"The promise of God is my portion"

Evening Prayer

Date: _____

Scripture:

Father I am believing for:

My Prayer

What God Said:

_____

_____

_____

_____

_____

_____

_____

_____

Evening journal dump!!
Write, Release, Restart

_____

_____

_____

_____

_____

_____

_____

_____

_____

_____

_____

_____

_____

Get Past The Past

Brethren, I count not myself to have apprehended: but this one thing I do, forgetting those things which are behind, and reaching forth unto those things which are before, I press toward the mark for the prize of the high calling of God in Christ Jesus.
Philippians 3:13-14

Now if we're being honest, it's not always those outside of us that are trying to pin us to our past. Sometimes we hold ourselves hostage to our past indiscretions either out of guilt, hurt, or shame. While forgiveness from those that feel we've wronged them is important, know that it is equally as important to forgive yourself. I can't tell you how many things I've held onto over the years while the other parties have moved on living their best lives and I'm over here punishing myself. If you know you have genuinely apologized and sought forgiveness move on. Even if it's not accepted. Keep in mind some people like the posture of victim and some withhold their forgiveness as a power play to keep you bound to the situation. Whatever the reason as long as you seek forgiveness from God in earnest it is forgiven. So, forgive yourself and leave it with God!

───────◆───────

Father today I am asking you for the will to forgive myself. Lord teach me how to love me the way you love me. Open my eyes so that I may see me as you see me. Father grant me the wisdom to know when to let go so that I may be free of the bondage of my past indiscretions and mistakes. Amen

Morning Prayer

Date: _____

Scripture:

Father I have faith you will:

My Prayer for revelation

What God Said:

_____
_____
_____
_____
_____
_____
_____

Daily Planner

DATE:

Things I need to accomplish today

- ○ _____
- ○ _____
- ○ _____
- ○ _____
- ○ _____
- ○ _____
- ○ _____
- ○ _____

Things I want to accomplish

Challenges I am prepared to face

Goals for Tomorrow

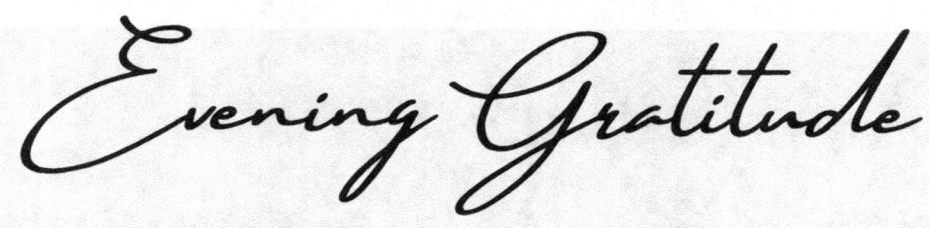

Evening Gratitude

Date: _____

Father Today I felt......

_____

_____

_____

Father I'm grateful for.....

_____

_____

_____

Father forgive me for.....

_____

_____

_____

Father as I close out today what can I do for you tomorrow...

_____

_____

_____

"The promise of God is my portion"

Evening Prayer

Date: _____

Scripture:

Father I am believing for:

My Prayer

What God Said:

_____

_____

_____

_____

_____

_____

_____

_____

Evening journal dump!!
Write, Release, Restart

_____

_____

_____

_____

_____

_____

_____

_____

_____

_____

_____

_____

_____

_____

Ordinary Deed
Extraordinary Outcome

So, when he had considered this, he came to the house of Mary, the mother of John whose surname was Mark, where many were gathered together praying.
Acts 12:12

Now this passage is talking about how Mary opened her doors to the people of God after Peter was arrested to give them a safe place to pray. They prayed and God eventually sent an angel to lead him out of prison. She did an ordinary thing and her simple act of kindness and obedience aided in the church's survival. Not everyone's path will lead them to leadership or some grand stage. Some of us are called to supporting positions, hospitality, security, service, etc. Whatever the vision for your life, know and understand that it is equally as important as any other role in this world. Some of us can lead simply by inviting others in!

━━━◆━━━

Lord let not my ego get in the way of whatever you have for me. Father let me see the value in me. I am grateful simply for the opportunity to be a part of your plan. Whatever you're doing Father please don't do it without me.

Amen

Morning Prayer

Date: _____

Scripture:

Father I have faith you will:

My Prayer for revelation

What God Said:

_____

_____

_____

_____

_____

_____

_____

DATE:

Daily Planner

Things I want to accomplish

Things I need to accomplish today

- ○ _____
- ○ _____
- ○ _____
- ○ _____
- ○ _____
- ○ _____
- ○ _____
- ○ _____

Challenges I am prepared to face

Goals for Tomorrow

Evening Gratitude

Date: _____

Father Today I felt......

_____

_____

_____

Father I'm grateful for.....

_____

_____

_____

Father forgive me for.....

_____

_____

_____

Father as I close out today what can I do for you tomorrow...

_____

_____

_____

"The promise of God is my portion"

Evening Prayer

Date: _____

Scripture:

Father I am believing for:

My Prayer

What God Said:

_____

_____

_____

_____

_____

_____

_____

Evening journal dump!!
Write, Release, Restart

_____

_____

_____

_____

_____

_____

_____

_____

_____

_____

_____

_____

_____

_____

_____

The Appointed Time

Now there was one, Anna, a prophetess, the daughter of Phanuel, of the tribe of Asher. She was of a great age, and had lived with a husband seven years from her virginity; and this woman was a widow of about eighty-four years, who did not depart from the temple, but served God with fastings and prayers night and day. And coming in that instant she gave thanks to the Lord, and spoke of Him to all those who looked for redemption in Jerusalem.
Luke 2:36-38

How many times have you become stagnant in your life? How many times has being in a posture of long suffering made you feel as if there was nothing good left for you in this life? Often times we can become complacent when we don't see instant results and this can lead to the belief that we no longer have a purpose, or we begin to believe we're too old to do great things. Anna is the perfect example of staying the course. She lost her husband after 7 years and remained a widow dedicated to serving God. She was steadfast in her service. God rewarded her by allowing her to witness baby Jesus! She then went out and shared the good news that redemption was coming. At 84 years old God gave her life new meaning. He had not forgotten her and still had a use and position for her in His plan. It's never too late to get what God has for you!

◆━━━━━━━━━◆

Father remind me when I am low in spirit that I am still your called and chosen vessel. Lord I thank you that failure is not my portion and there is a place for me in your kingdom. Amen

Morning Prayer

Date: _____

Scripture:

Father I have faith you will:

My Prayer for revelation

What God Said:

_____

_____

_____

_____

_____

_____

_____

DATE:

Daily Planner

Things I want to accomplish

Things I need to accomplish today

- ⭘ _____
- ⭘ _____
- ⭘ _____
- ⭘ _____
- ⭘ _____
- ⭘ _____
- ⭘ _____
- ⭘ _____

Challenges I am prepared to face

Goals for Tomorrow

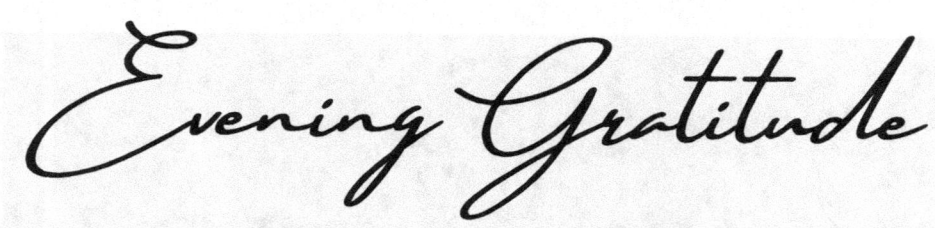

Evening Gratitude

Date: _____

Father Today I felt......

_____

_____

_____

Father I'm grateful for.....

_____

_____

_____

Father forgive me for.....

_____

_____

_____

Father as I close out today what can I do for you tomorrow...

_____

_____

_____

"The promise of God is my portion"

Evening Prayer

Date: _____

Scripture:
Father I am believing for:

My Prayer

What God Said:

_____

_____

_____

_____

_____

_____

_____

_____

Evening journal dump!!
Write, Release, Restart

_____

_____

_____

_____

_____

_____

_____

_____

_____

_____

_____

_____

_____

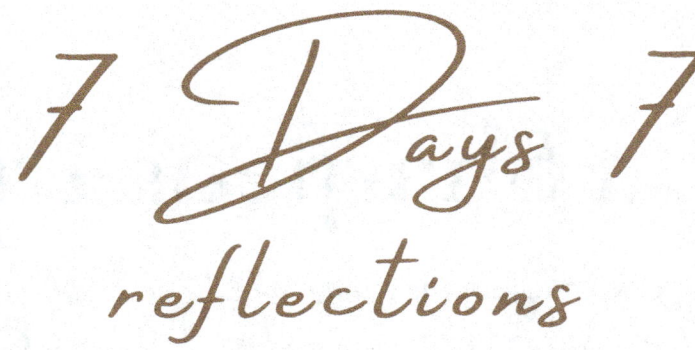

7 Days 7

reflections

MONDAY

TUESDAY

WEDNESDAY

THURSDAY

FRIDAY

SATURDAY

SUNDAY

Iron Sharpens Iron

So he began to speak boldly in the synagogue. When Aquila and Priscilla heard him, they took him aside and explained to him the way of God more accurately. And when he desired to cross to Achaia, the brethren wrote, exhorting the disciples to receive him; and when he arrived, he greatly helped those who had believed through grace.
Acts 18:26-27

This text references Apollos, a man who spoke eloquently and mighty in the scriptures. However, in order for him to reach more people, God created a divine connection between him and two others that had a different level of knowledge to impart into him. Because he was receptive, he was able to spread the gospel to an entirely new territory. In order for God to truly launch His vison for your life you must be teachable and reachable. You won't have all the answers all the time. So, when God orchestrates divine connections, it is to ensure you remain fruitful and productive. If you are unable to be taught or to follow, how can you teach or lead?

◆━━━━━◆

Lord help me to be teachable. Let my heart and mind be good ground so that seeds sown into me may take root. Father grant me the wisdom to discern between those you have assigned to me and imposters so that I may bear good fruit. Amen

Morning Prayer

Date: _____

Scripture:

Father I have faith you will:

My Prayer for revelation

What God Said:

_____

_____

_____

_____

_____

_____

_____

_____

DATE:

Daily Planner

Things I want to accomplish

Things I need to accomplish today

- ⚪ _____
- ⚪ _____
- ⚪ _____
- ⚪ _____
- ⚪ _____
- ⚪ _____
- ⚪ _____
- ⚪ _____

Challenges I am prepared to face

Goals for Tomorrow

Evening Gratitude

Date: _____

Father Today I felt......

_____

_____

_____

Father I'm grateful for.....

_____

_____

_____

Father forgive me for.....

_____

_____

_____

Father as I close out today what can I do for you tomorrow...

_____

_____

_____

"The promise of God is my portion"

Date: _____

Scripture:

Father I am believing for:

My Prayer

What God Said:

_____

_____

_____

_____

_____

_____

_____

Evening journal dump!!
Write, Release, Restart

_____

_____

_____

_____

_____

_____

_____

_____

_____

_____

_____

_____

No Competition

Then Miriam and Aaron spoke against Moses because of the Ethiopian woman whom he had married; for he had married an Ethiopian woman. So they said, "Has the Lord indeed spoken only through Moses? Has He not spoken through us also?" and the Lord heard it.
Numbers 12:1-2

Miriam was a great and wise woman in her own rite. However, she allowed envy and ego to make her question her position but also to covet the position of Moses. It's a fact of life that with new levels come new devils. Don't spend one ounce of time focused on what the next sister is doing. Your vision will be personal to your gifting, just as hers is personal to hers. Your gifting will make room for you as long as you are willing to do the work and stay the course. Avoid sharing everything with everyone. Miriam allowed outside influences to skew her view of her brother and it cost her something. God eventually restored her, but it could have been avoided. Not everyone who wishes you well actually wishes you well!!!

◆——————◆

Lord search my heart and cleanse me of any ill feelings toward my sister. Father help me keep at the forefront of my mind that my sister is not my adversary but my partner in the kingdom. Give me a heart to support and serve so that I may be supported and served when the times comes. Amen

Morning Prayer

Date: _____

Scripture:

Father I have faith you will:

My Prayer for revelation

What God Said:

_____

_____

_____

_____

_____

_____

_____

Daily Planner

Things I want to accomplish

Things I need to accomplish today

- ⃝ _____
- ⃝ _____
- ⃝ _____
- ⃝ _____
- ⃝ _____
- ⃝ _____
- ⃝ _____
- ⃝ _____

Challenges I am prepared to face

Goals for Tomorrow

Evening Gratitude

Date: _____

Father Today I felt......

_____
_____
_____

Father I'm grateful for.....

_____
_____
_____

Father forgive me for.....

_____
_____
_____

Father as I close out today what can I do for you tomorrow...

_____
_____
_____

"The promise of God is my portion"

Date: _____

Scripture:

Father I am believing for:

My Prayer

What God Said:

_____

_____

_____

_____

_____

_____

_____

Evening journal dump!!
Write, Release, Restart

_____

_____

_____

_____

_____

_____

_____

_____

_____

_____

_____

The Path

Trust in the Lord with all your heart and lean not on your own understanding; in all your ways submit to him, and he will make your paths straight.
Proverbs 3:5-6

DAY

When you get in your car you usually have a destination in mind. If you're like myself, you keep the Maps app handy in case you lose your way. On this journey you will need to seek the Holy Spirit to confirm your destination. Once you have that continue to use God as your navigation. There's no guarantee that it will be a straight path; very few roads we travel are.

Father God I am ready. Direct my path, where you lead me, I will follow. Amen

Morning Prayer

Date: _____

Scripture:

Father I have faith you will:

My Prayer for revelation

What God Said:

_____
_____
_____
_____
_____
_____
_____
_____

Daily Planner

Things I need to accomplish today

- ○ _____
- ○ _____
- ○ _____
- ○ _____
- ○ _____
- ○ _____
- ○ _____
- ○ _____

Things I want to accomplish

Goals for Tomorrow

Challenges I am prepared to face

Evening Gratitude

Date: _____

Father Today I felt......

_____

_____

_____

Father I'm grateful for.....

_____

_____

_____

Father forgive me for.....

_____

_____

_____

Father as I close out today what can I do for you tomorrow...

_____

_____

_____

"The promise of God is my portion"

Evening Prayer

Date: _____

Scripture:

Father I am believing for:

My Prayer

What God Said:

_____

_____

_____

_____

_____

_____

_____

Evening journal dump!!
Write, Release, Restart

_____

_____

_____

_____

_____

_____

_____

_____

_____

_____

_____

_____

Wisdom is Strategy

The fear of the Lord is the beginning of knowledge, but fools despise wisdom and instruction.
Proverbs 1:7

In order to execute a solid plan, you must first have a solid strategy. In order to birth a great strategy, you must operate in and with wisdom. In this scripture, wisdom is the fear of the Lord. Not a cower in the corner type of fear, but a posture in which you exalt His counsel over your own. You trust that what God instructs you to do is what's best for you.

Lord help me to adjust my posture to that of fear and reverence of you. Give me the strength to trust in you, Amen

Morning Prayer

Date: _____

Scripture:

Father I have faith you will:

My Prayer for revelation

What God Said:

_____
_____
_____
_____
_____
_____
_____
_____

Daily Planner

DATE:

Things I want to accomplish

Things I need to accomplish today

- ○ _____
- ○ _____
- ○ _____
- ○ _____
- ○ _____
- ○ _____
- ○ _____
- ○ _____

Challenges I am prepared to face

Goals for Tomorrow

Evening Gratitude

Date: _____

Father Today I felt……

_____

_____

_____

Father I'm grateful for…..

_____

_____

_____

Father forgive me for…..

_____

_____

_____

Father as I close out today what can I do for you tomorrow…

_____

_____

_____

"The promise of God is my portion"

Evening Prayer

Date: _____

Scripture:

Father I am believing for:

My Prayer

What God Said:

_____
_____
_____
_____
_____
_____
_____

Evening journal dump!!
Write, Release, Restart

Wisdoms Warning

Wisdom calls aloud outside; She raises her voice in the open squares. She cries out in the chief concourses, At the openings of the gates in the city She speaks her words: How long, you simple ones, will you love simplicity? For scorners delight in their scorning, And fools hate knowledge.
Proverbs 1:20-22

Being patient and waiting for the answers you seek is wise. Sometimes the excitement of what we believe is to come can cloud our judgement and lead us to make rushed uniformed decisions. This is a labor of love, a birthing process. It must be entered into with care. Each piece uniquely designed to fit seamlessly together as a whole. It is an extension of you and a reflection of who you are in God, and proof of your obedience.

Father I patiently await your answers and heed the warnings. Amen

Morning Prayer

Date: _____

Scripture:

Father I have faith you will:

My Prayer for revelation

What God Said:

_____

_____

_____

_____

_____

_____

_____

_____

Daily Planner

Things I need to accomplish today

- ○ _____
- ○ _____
- ○ _____
- ○ _____
- ○ _____
- ○ _____
- ○ _____
- ○ _____

Things I want to accomplish

Goals for Tomorrow

Challenges I am prepared to face

Date: _____

Father Today I felt......

_____

_____

_____

Father I'm grateful for.....

_____

_____

_____

Father forgive me for.....

_____

_____

_____

Father as I close out today what can I do for you tomorrow...

_____

_____

_____

"The promise of God is my portion"

Evening Prayer

Date: _____

Scripture:

Father I am believing for:

My Prayer

What God Said:

_____

_____

_____

_____

_____

_____

_____

Evening journal dump!!
Write, Release, Restart

_____

_____

_____

_____

_____

_____

_____

_____

_____

_____

_____

_____

A Good Steward

Go from the presence of a foolish man, When you do not perceive in him the lips of knowledge. The wisdom of the prudent is to understand his way, But the folly of fools is deceit.
Proverbs 14:7-8

Here's the thing, we are all allotted the same number of hours in a day. What we do with that time will ultimately dictate what we get out of it. In order to be productive, you must manage your resources well. Time is a resource. Be conscious of your decisions and your state of mind when making them. Remember everyone cannot speak to God's vision for you, so don't waste time looking for outside validation. Stick to the plan!!
Better yet, stick to His plan!!

$\longleftrightarrow$

Lord give me the wisdom to be a good steward over all that you have blessed me with. Guide me to manage my resources in well.

Amen

Morning Prayer

Date: _____

> **Scripture:**
>
> Father I have faith you will:

My Prayer for revelation

What God Said:

_____

_____

_____

_____

_____

_____

_____

DATE:

Daily Planner

Things I need to accomplish today

- ○ _____
- ○ _____
- ○ _____
- ○ _____
- ○ _____
- ○ _____
- ○ _____
- ○ _____

Things I want to accomplish

Goals for Tomorrow

Challenges I am prepared to face

Evening Gratitude

Date: _____

Father Today I felt......

_____

_____

_____

Father I'm grateful for.....

_____

_____

_____

Father forgive me for.....

_____

_____

_____

Father as I close out today what can I do for you tomorrow...

_____

_____

_____

"The promise of God is my portion"

Evening Prayer

Date: _____

Scripture:

Father I am believing for:

My Prayer

What God Said:

_____

_____

_____

_____

_____

_____

_____

Evening journal dump!!
Write, Release, Restart

_____

_____

_____

_____

_____

_____

_____

_____

_____

_____

_____

_____

_____

Pour or Poor

For by wise counsel you will wage your own war, And in a multitude of counselors there is safety. Wisdom is too lofty for a fool; He does not open his mouth in the gate.
Proverbs 24:6-7

I heard a word from a very wise young lady not too long ago. She said, "Poor people can't afford anything but an epiphany." and she's right. There are 2 types of "poor" folks. The first type are those who pour, as in providing wise counsel, encouragement, covering, accountability, sowing into, and uplifting others. Those are the people you can be certain God has aligned you with. Then there are the "poor" folks, they lack good judgment, aren't good stewards over what they have/had, aren't productive, are constantly going through something, never take accountability, and will never hold you accountable. Not everyone's moral compass is calibrated to the direction God may be leading you. This is why being intentional when seeking wise counsel is important. The right circle and connections will almost guarantee your success. It's ok to accept the wisdom of others to help us along the way to our goal or vision. I believe that God creates these divine connections so we have an advantage when we connect with one another.

Lord I want to pour and connect to those who pour. Grant me wisdom so that I may never be poor. Amen

Morning Prayer

Date: _____

Scripture:

Father I have faith you will:

My Prayer for revelation

What God Said:

_____
_____
_____
_____
_____
_____
_____
_____

DATE:

Daily Planner

Things I want to accomplish

Things I need to accomplish today

- ○ _____
- ○ _____
- ○ _____
- ○ _____
- ○ _____
- ○ _____
- ○ _____
- ○ _____

Goals for Tomorrow

Challenges I am prepared to face

Evening Gratitude

Date: _____

Father Today I felt......

_____

_____

_____

Father I'm grateful for.....

_____

_____

_____

Father forgive me for.....

_____

_____

_____

Father as I close out today what can I do for you tomorrow...

_____

_____

_____

"The promise of God is my portion"

Evening Prayer

Date: _____

Scripture:

Father I am believing for:

My Prayer

What God Said:

_____

_____

_____

_____

_____

_____

_____

Evening journal dump!!
Write, Release, Restart

_____

_____

_____

_____

_____

_____

_____

_____

_____

_____

_____

_____

_____

7 Days 7 reflections

MONDAY

TUESDAY

WEDNESDAY

THURSDAY

FRIDAY

SATURDAY

SUNDAY

Even The Worst of You

And we know that all things work together for good to those who love God, to those who are called according to His purpose.
Romans 8:28

DAY

This one is simple. Yes, even the parts of you that you may feel are not the best or the world deems not good enough, God will use them for your good. There is no part of you that is so damaged, broken, or irreparable that no good can come from it. We all have a redemption song in our hearts. Every bad experience I've ever had God has shown me purpose in them. Those experiences are what led you to me and to this book. He took my POOR and turned it into a POUR! We are His perfect imperfection.

Lord thank you for choosing me. Amen

Morning Prayer

Date: _____

Scripture:

Father I have faith you will:

My Prayer for revelation

What God Said:

_____

_____

_____

_____

_____

_____

_____

_____

DATE:

Daily Planner

Things I want to accomplish

Things I need to accomplish today

- ○ _____
- ○ _____
- ○ _____
- ○ _____
- ○ _____
- ○ _____
- ○ _____
- ○ _____

Challenges I am prepared to face

Goals for Tomorrow

Evening Gratitude

Date: _____

Father Today I felt......

_____

_____

_____

Father I'm grateful for.....

_____

_____

_____

Father forgive me for.....

_____

_____

_____

Father as I close out today what can I do for you tomorrow...

_____

_____

_____

"The promise of God is my portion"

Evening Prayer

Date: _____

Scripture:

Father I am believing for:

My Prayer

What God Said:

_____

_____

_____

_____

_____

_____

_____

_____

Evening journal dump!!
Write, Release, Restart

_____

_____

_____

_____

_____

_____

_____

_____

_____

_____

_____

_____

_____

_____

Set Apart Not Above

But the manifestation of the Spirit is given to each one for the profit of all: for to one is given the word of wisdom through the Spirit, to another the word of knowledge through the same Spirit, to another faith by the same Spirit, to another gifts of healings by the same Spirit, to another the working of miracles, to another prophecy, to another discerning of spirits, to another different kinds of tongues, to another the interpretation of tongues. But one and the same Spirit works all these things, distributing to each one individually as He wills.
1 Corinthians 12:7-11

Launching your vision can be exhilarating. It can leave you feeling empowered or give you a feeling of validation, but what we must all remember is that each of our individual gifts serves a collective purpose and that purpose is the people we SERVE. Always keep in the forefront of your mind the gift although manifesting through you is NOT yours personally but God's. He has charged you with those assigned to you. Your gift should help them in some way, never hurt them. Be mindful not to become haughty or puffed up, your gift should not separate you from the people but serve to bring you closer to them in some way.

——————◆——————

Lord help me to stay the course and be the extension of you that you desire for me to be. Teach me to be a good steward over those assigned to me so that I may be a help and not a hinderance.   Amen

Morning Prayer

Date: _____

Scripture:

Father I have faith you will:

My Prayer for revelation

What God Said:

_____

_____

_____

_____

_____

_____

_____

Daily Planner

Things I need to accomplish today

- ○ _____
- ○ _____
- ○ _____
- ○ _____
- ○ _____
- ○ _____
- ○ _____
- ○ _____

Things I want to accomplish

Challenges I am prepared to face

Goals for Tomorrow

Evening Gratitude

Date: _____

Father Today I felt......

_____

_____

_____

Father I'm grateful for.....

_____

_____

_____

Father forgive me for.....

_____

_____

_____

Father as I close out today what can I do for you tomorrow...

_____

_____

_____

"The promise of God is my portion"

Evening Prayer

Date: _____

Scripture:

Father I am believing for:

My Prayer

What God Said:

_____

_____

_____

_____

_____

_____

_____

_____

Evening journal dump!!
Write, Release, Restart

Heart work is Hard work

DAY

We have all heard the saying "*anything worth having is worth working for*". In order to truly be successful, you must put in the effort. Food always tastes better when it's prepared with love! This is true when building your vision. How do you want to be perceived and received? If you are sloppy, cut corners, and use subpar materials, your foundation will not be firm and at some point, it will crumble. Be intentional about the effort you put in. Do not become impatient and hasty as you will make mistakes. Also, don't dwell on past mistakes it's ok to remember but don't get stuck there. Be original and authentic at every stage. You want longevity. Ask yourself what you want your legacy to be and then get to work.

Lord today I am looking ahead with a spirit of gladness, I will not dwell in the past, I will move forward as you have. I am willing to do the work. Amen

Morning Prayer

Date: _____

Scripture:

Father I have faith you will:

My Prayer for revelation

What God Said:

_____
_____
_____
_____
_____
_____
_____
_____

DATE:

Daily Planner

Things I want to accomplish

Things I need to accomplish today

- ○ _____
- ○ _____
- ○ _____
- ○ _____
- ○ _____
- ○ _____
- ○ _____
- ○ _____

Challenges I am prepared to face

Goals for Tomorrow

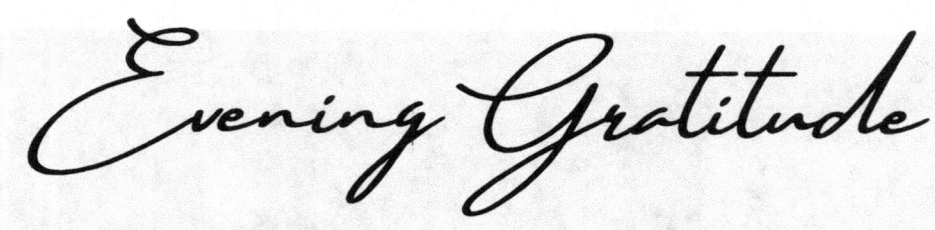

Evening Gratitude

Date: _____

Father Today I felt......

_____
_____
_____

Father I'm grateful for.....

_____
_____
_____

Father forgive me for.....

_____
_____
_____

Father as I close out today what can I do for you tomorrow...

_____
_____
_____

"The promise of God is my portion"

Evening Prayer

Date: _____

Scripture:

Father I am believing for:

My Prayer

What God Said:

_____

_____

_____

_____

_____

_____

_____

Evening journal dump!!
Write, Release, Restart

_____

_____

_____

_____

_____

_____

_____

_____

_____

_____

_____

_____

_____

Keep Moving

And let us not grow weary while doing good, for in due season we shall reap if we do not lose heart.
Galatians 6:9

DAY

I would be lying if I told you this process would go smoothly. It won't. There will be times when you get frustrated, feel defeated, or even feel like giving up. If you are fully persuaded by what God has revealed to you, then you know He has not set you up to fail. Take your moment, give it to Him in prayer, and move forward. If it's an answer you seek, then take a break and wait for His response but don't let the little inconveniences deter you from the big picture.

Father when I am frustrated, help me to move past it and readjust my posture. Amen

Morning Prayer

Date: _____

Scripture:

Father I have faith you will:

My Prayer for revelation

What God Said:

_____

_____

_____

_____

_____

_____

_____

Daily Planner

DATE:

Things I need to accomplish today

- ○ _____
- ○ _____
- ○ _____
- ○ _____
- ○ _____
- ○ _____
- ○ _____
- ○ _____

Things I want to accomplish

Challenges I am prepared to face

Goals for Tomorrow

Evening Gratitude

Date: _____

Father Today I felt......

_____

_____

_____

Father I'm grateful for.....

_____

_____

_____

Father forgive me for.....

_____

_____

_____

Father as I close out today what can I do for you tomorrow...

_____

_____

_____

"The promise of God is my portion"

Evening Prayer

Date: _____

Scripture:

Father I am believing for:

My Prayer

What God Said:

_____

_____

_____

_____

_____

_____

_____

Evening journal dump!!
Write, Release, Restart

It's True

And I also say to you that you are Peter, and on this rock I will build My church, and the gates of Hades shall not prevail against it.
Matthew 16:18

DAY

As women we are preprogrammed to be dependent, often told we need the help of others to accomplish anything that is not deemed by the world "women's work". It can be difficult to overcome that thought process and push past social barriers. The point is not to make you rebel against certain traditions, but to encourage you to start new ones. God wants to do a new thing in this season and YES SIS, HE CHOSE YOU!!

Lord it can be hard to go against the grain, help me to push through, settle in my spirit that you did in fact choose me. Amen

Morning Prayer

Date: _____

Scripture:

Father I have faith you will:

My Prayer for revelation

What God Said:

_____

_____

_____

_____

_____

_____

_____

Daily Planner

DATE:

Things I need to accomplish today

- ○ _____
- ○ _____
- ○ _____
- ○ _____
- ○ _____
- ○ _____
- ○ _____
- ○ _____

Things I want to accomplish

Challenges I am prepared to face

Goals for Tomorrow

Evening Gratitude

Date: _____

Father Today I felt......

_____

_____

_____

Father I'm grateful for.....

_____

_____

_____

Father forgive me for.....

_____

_____

_____

Father as I close out today what can I do for you tomorrow...

_____

_____

_____

"The promise of God is my portion"

Evening Prayer

Date: _____

Scripture:

Father I am believing for:

My Prayer

What God Said:

_____

_____

_____

_____

_____

_____

Evening journal dump!!
Write, Release, Restart

_____

_____

_____

_____

_____

_____

_____

_____

_____

_____

_____

_____

_____

_____

Opposition Will Come

The Lord will fight for you; you need only to be still."
Exodus 14:14

When God called you, it was not a conference call. Everyone won't be receptive to your vision. There will always be those naysayers, offering criticism without solutions. You will have those who can't get past a certain version of you in their minds, accusing you of being out of line or telling you that you are not ready. Be still! Do not engage. The truth of the matter is they just aren't ready to let you go or grow. You see some people don't mind feeding you from the table because they control the portion. Do not get yourself worked up and NO you do not have to defend yourself. Be still and let God do what He does best!!!

Father help me to be still, be proactive instead of reactive. Amen

Morning Prayer

Date: _____

Scripture:

Father I have faith you will:

My Prayer for revelation

What God Said:

_____
_____
_____
_____
_____
_____
_____

Daily Planner

Things I want to accomplish

Things I need to accomplish today

- ○ _____
- ○ _____
- ○ _____
- ○ _____
- ○ _____
- ○ _____
- ○ _____
- ○ _____

Challenges I am prepared to face

Goals for Tomorrow

Evening Gratitude

Date: _____

Father Today I felt......

_____

_____

_____

Father I'm grateful for.....

_____

_____

_____

Father forgive me for.....

_____

_____

_____

Father as I close out today what can I do for you tomorrow...

_____

_____

_____

"The promise of God is my portion"

Evening Prayer

Date: _____

Scripture:

Father I am believing for:

My Prayer

What God Said:

_____

_____

_____

_____

_____

_____

_____

Evening journal dump!!
Write, Release, Restart

_____

_____

_____

_____

_____

_____

_____

_____

_____

_____

_____

_____

_____

It's Already Done

You prepare a table before me in the presence of my enemies; You anoint my head with oil; My cup runs over.
Psalm 23:5

DAY

One thing for sure, God is not a man that He should lie. He said it and He meant it. The table WILL BE SET! When HE is ready, at the appointed time, He will build the table that is for YOU!

Lord thank you. Amen

Morning Prayer

Date: _____

Scripture:

Father I have faith you will:

My Prayer for revelation

What God Said:

_____

_____

_____

_____

_____

_____

_____

_____

Daily Planner

DATE:

Things I want to accomplish

Things I need to accomplish today

- ⭕ _____
- ⭕ _____
- ⭕ _____
- ⭕ _____
- ⭕ _____
- ⭕ _____
- ⭕ _____
- ⭕ _____

Challenges I am prepared to face

Goals for Tomorrow

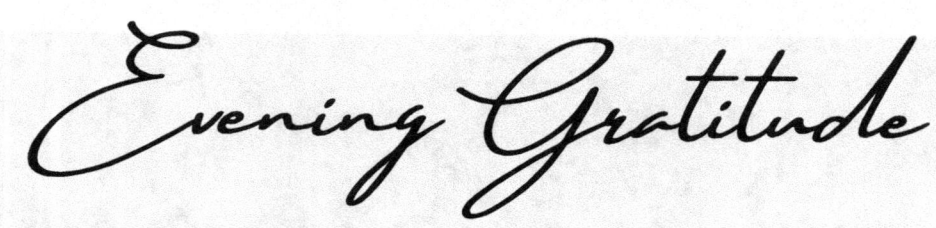

Evening Gratitude

Date: _____

Father Today I felt......

_____

_____

_____

Father I'm grateful for.....

_____

_____

_____

Father forgive me for.....

_____

_____

_____

Father as I close out today what can I do for you tomorrow...

_____

_____

_____

"The promise of God is my portion"

Evening Prayer

Date: _____

Scripture:

Father I am believing for:

My Prayer

What God Said:

_____

_____

_____

_____

_____

_____

_____

Evening journal dump!!
Write, Release, Restart

_____

_____

_____

_____

_____

_____

_____

_____

_____

_____

_____

_____

_____

7 Days 7 reflections

MONDAY

TUESDAY

WEDNESDAY

THURSDAY

FRIDAY

SATURDAY

SUNDAY

And I Can

"Go, gather all the Jews who are present in Shushan, and fast for me; neither eat nor drink for three days, night or day. My maids and I will fast likewise. And so I will go to the king, which is against the law; and if I perish, I perish!"
Esther 4:16

DAY

Can I just tell you how powerful this statement is!!! When Queen Esther decided that she was ready to go to war for the vision God had for her she did so knowing it could cost her her life! That is a measure of courage that you will have to tap into in order to successfully launch your vision. Is it worth fighting for? Courage, determination and persistence are already in us. Tap in. Have the courage to fight for YOU and what you know God promised you. This is your opportunity, you are worth it and I want to see you win!

◆━━━━━━━◆

Lord I can do all things through and with you. I bind the spirit of fear, anxiety and low self esteem. I am powerful in you. Amen

Morning Prayer

Date: _____

Scripture:

Father I have faith you will:

My Prayer for revelation

What God Said:

_____
_____
_____
_____
_____
_____
_____

Daily Planner

DATE:

Things I need to accomplish today

- ○ _____
- ○ _____
- ○ _____
- ○ _____
- ○ _____
- ○ _____
- ○ _____
- ○ _____

Things I want to accomplish

Goals for Tomorrow

Challenges I am prepared to face

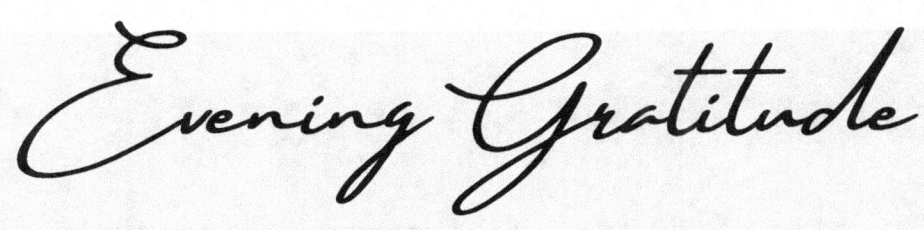

Evening Gratitude

Date: _____

Father Today I felt......

_____

_____

_____

Father I'm grateful for.....

_____

_____

_____

Father forgive me for.....

_____

_____

_____

Father as I close out today what can I do for you tomorrow...

_____

_____

_____

"The promise of God is my portion"

Evening Prayer

Date: _____

Scripture:

Father I am believing for:

My Prayer

What God Said:

_____

_____

_____

_____

_____

_____

_____

Evening journal dump!!
Write, Release, Restart

_____

_____

_____

_____

_____

_____

_____

_____

_____

_____

_____

_____

You Can't Imagine

Then the angel said to her, "Do not be afraid, Mary, for you have found favor with God. And behold, you will conceive in your womb and bring forth a Son, and shall call His name JESUS.
Luke 1:30-31

Can you imagine what it was like for Mary, to be pregnant but not by her husband? One can only imagine the ridicule and speculation she must have endured. She made a great sacrifice. It had to have been a lonely place to be for no one to understand why God chose her or what His purpose for her was. God truly used her, and she ended up giving birth to the light of the world, a King, the Son of God. No matter how trying the process was, the end result was worth every tear she cried and just like Mary, despite the pressing, continue to stand and watch what God has got in store for you!!!

Lord I'm trusting and believing you even in the low moments. Uncertainty will not steal my joy Amen

Morning Prayer

Date: _____

Scripture:

Father I have faith you will:

My Prayer for revelation

What God Said:

_____
_____
_____
_____
_____
_____
_____
_____

Daily Planner

Things I want to accomplish

Things I need to accomplish today

- ○ _____
- ○ _____
- ○ _____
- ○ _____
- ○ _____
- ○ _____
- ○ _____
- ○ _____

Challenges I am prepared to face

Goals for Tomorrow

Evening Gratitude

Date: _____

Father Today I felt......

_____

_____

_____

Father I'm grateful for.....

_____

_____

_____

Father forgive me for.....

_____

_____

_____

Father as I close out today what can I do for you tomorrow...

_____

_____

_____

"The promise of God is my portion"

Date: _____

Scripture:

Father I am believing for:

My Prayer

What God Said:

_____

_____

_____

_____

_____

_____

_____

Evening journal dump!!
Write, Release, Restart

Yaaassss Sis!

FINISH

Now that you've reached the end of this journey, you may be wondering what's next!! Well Sit tight because God is definitely not done with you yet. Getting to know yourself is only a small part in emerging into who God called you to be. Over the last 30days you have also been building a better relationship with him by improving your prayer life, using him as your shoulder to cry out in the 5 min melt down and learning about the things that have been weighing you down mentally with the mental health minute. All of these things are building blocks in the foundation of manifesting the vision. They are helping you develop self discipline, consistency, and self awareness all things necessary to manage any calling on your life. Take a moment to celebrate how far you've come. Give yourself a moment to revel in Gods heart for you and treat yourself to something special and when you're ready go grab the next guide in this series! Remember I am on this journey with you.

I AM THE MASTERPIECE

20_VISION

BOARD

Launch The Vision, Sis!